This Book Belongs to:

_____

D1507243

C is for Chafing

TO BEATRICE
Who teaches me every day
that "Bea" is for Beautiful

And special thanks to
Sarah and Warren Greene,
for inspiring
"I is for Ice bath"

C is for Chafing

Mark Remy

Illustrations by Eric Cash

Running is a *special* thing,
It's very plain to see

Running is a *healthy* thing,
Good for you and me

Running can be *scary*, too,
Like when you scrape your knee

But mostly it's *enjoyable* –
Fun from A to Z!

A is for Against traffic

The safest way to run

B is for Blister

Owie! That's no fun

C is for Chafing

Inner thighs are burning

D is for DNF

His G.I. tract is churning

E is for Endorphins

They fuel the runner's high

F is for Fartlek

(That's "speed play," by the by)

G is for

Get off the road!

Respect's a two-way street

H is for Hopkinton

Where Boston runners meet

I is for Ice bath

Daddy's teeth sure chatter!

J is for Jogger

Slow? It doesn't matter.

K is for Kenya

Where kids all ages run

L is for Love

Their journey's just begun

M is for Marathon

That medal is a dandy

N is for Nipple

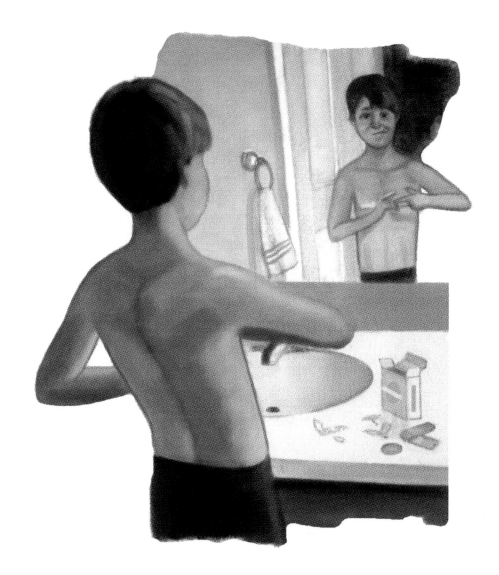

These things come in handy

O is for "Oh, no..."

This means you ran too hard

P is for Pasta

A runner's source of carbs

Q is for Quarters

Repeats make you fast-y

R is for Roadkill

Phew! That sure smells nasty!

S is for Spectator

A big source of support

T is for Treadmill

Used as a last resort

U is for

Underdeveloped
upper body

Fast guys have sunken chests

V is for VO_2 max

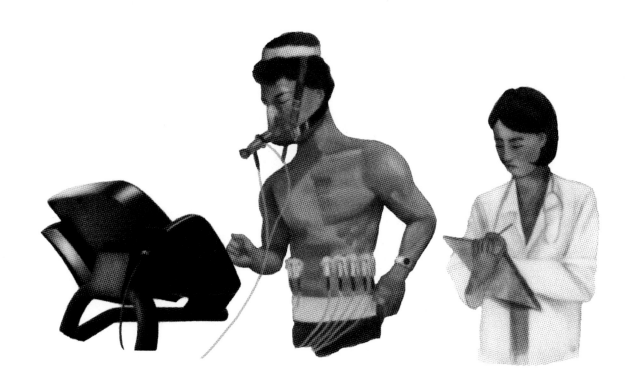

King of the fitness tests

W is for Water

Drink only when you're thirsty

X is for X-country

Plan on getting dirty

Y is for Yikes

CATEGORY B - RM 200 Per Entry		
EVENTS	Early Bird (1st Feb-31st March)	
Full Marathon	130.00	
	145.00	

How much? Can that be true?

Z is for Zzzz...

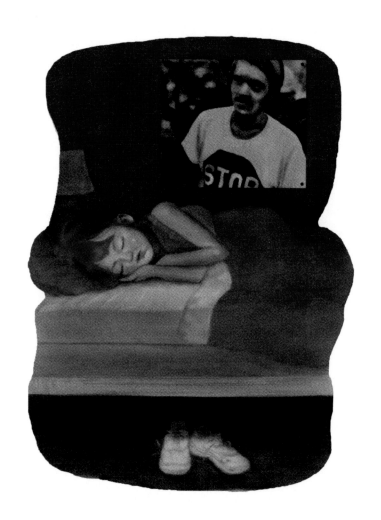

'Cause rest is training, too!

ABOUT THE AUTHOR

Mark Remy is a writer, editor, and runner in Pennsylvania's
Lehigh Valley, where he lives with his wife and daughter.

His previous *books* are *The Runner's Rule Book* (Rodale, 2009)
and *The Runner's Field Manual* (Rodale, 2010).

~

Eric Cash is a retro-style illustrator and portrait artist
who lives in Dallas with his wife, Misty, and two children,
Ethan and Emma. To see more of his work,
visit www.ericcashillustration.com.

Made in the USA
San Bernardino, CA
16 December 2017